Cannot Be Broken

Cannot Be Broken

Anshupriya Singh

UNICORN BOOKS
www.unicornbooks.in • info@unicornbooks.in

Unicorn Books
F-2/16, Ansari Road,
Darya Ganj, New Delhi-110002, India.

First Edition, May 2023

ISBN No. 978-81-7806-580-9

Preface

"To be a poet is a condition, not a profession."

So true to say. Writing is something I pursued as a hobby. Though I loved writing poems, publishing a book wasn't really I thought about.

People have their own ways to express themselves and for me it was through writing. To pen down what is moving in my head, and to give my thoughts a flow and rhythm, to mould them into words is another kind of experience.

Truly, for me poetry itself is a language. But honestly, it's just not me but my father as well whose genes I have acquired. Because it's he who arose in me the curiosity through his own works of writing.

For me, a book being published of my own wasn't a destination to reach but a journey that I enjoyed.

The strength that kept me going on this journey was always from my family. My mother has always been an inspiration for what I have done and sought to do. Having younger siblings is not just a responsibility but having systems to support you and cheer you up at your lows, and so were mine.

Like every other fairy tale, I got my fairy gods in the form of my Nana-Nani and Mama and my grandparents. Without them, the journey was truly unimaginable.

But the second half of me is dedicated to my school, Arvind Gupta D.A.V. Centenary Public School and to my teachers without the support and guidance of whom I was next to nothing. I am very grateful to Principal Mam, Ms. Mala Sood for providing me with enormous opportunities to prove myself. I am also thankful to my class teacher Ms. Rajni Mahajan, who's the actual reason behind my excellence.

Not every day is alike, some are as good as blooming flowers and others could be as bad as falling leaves. But the beauty lies in both. I could have never realised this beauty until my friends came to my life. Having a squad, who understand and appreciate is truly overwhelming. I am grateful to every single person who have been a part of my journey.

'Cannot Be Broken' is a collection of few of my works. Through this, I want to represent not just myself but every other teenager out there who feels the same way as I do at some point of time in life. May be it's my way to connect to you.

Enjoy reading!

— *Anshupriya Singh*

Contents

□□□

For The World To Adorn

Next to nothing,
Like a pore it was
Gradually growing inside the walls.

Without a clue,
About the world outside
Experiencing time and perceiving tide.

Yet another moment,
Fighting to be free
Waiting for the world to sense the gee.

Unknowing,
Of the aroma around
How soothing the womb was found!

Lay before,
A newly concepted world
Trying the senses to uphold.

To the glory,
A life was born
For the world to adorn.

❑❑❑

You Don't Know

You don't know the deepness
Of that room
You don't know about the tales
Carved on that wall,
You don't know how many times that quilt
Have been the escape for my tears
You don't know how often the moon
Has watched me budge.

You don't know, because what you see is
Majestic rooms,
High walls,
And expensive quilts.

You don't know how the leaves of that diary
Have understood the story of my days
You don't know how often that pen has filled in me
The spark of enthusiasm,
You don't know how that wooden desk has given
Sky to my dreams
You don't know how that chair has managed to gear up
My exhausted soul.

You don't know, because what you see is
The bunch of books,
And the imported chairs.

You don't know how many failures approached
Before that success
You don't know about the countless tears
Behind that smile,

You don't know about the sleepless nights
That back those bright eyes
You don't know about the drops of sweat
That accompanied me to stand proud.

You don't know, because what you see is
The joy of success,
The smile,
And the head held high.

You don't know how often the clothes
Were soaked in sweat
You don't know about the foot blisters
That occurred prior those boots,
You don't know how I have carved the lines
On my palm myself
You don't know that every time
The fortune hasn't worked.

You don't know, because what you see is
Expensive clothes,
And high priced boots,
The gentle hands,
And the faithful luck.
How effortlessly you put the strings of my abilities
In the hands of fortune
How you just define my luck to be good
Without giving a thought full.

It is because you don't know!

❐❐❐

Attraction Is Not Always Great

Those boyhood days seem so awkward,
When you hate yourself more than ever.
You have to be cool to be in trend,
And that is why it became my friend.

Those strange feelings and awkwardness,
And I had the fear of missing out.
And that pulled me towards itself,
Was I influenced by my own self?

Initially coughing and coughing hard,
Getting used to
Other fashion may not work because.

Nothing but a lighter was found in,
I was hardly scolded that night.
When others of my age were doing the same,
Was that a crime that I assumed to be a way to fame.

A stress burster it was now,
Turning habits into addiction.
My decision was right, I was sure,
But who knows, addiction don't have cures.

That soothing smoke was now a river of blood,
That stress burster was now a reason of depression.
The popular guy was now a fellow ignored,
When realisation hits in the deep core.

A lesson I learnt, I learnt so late,
Attraction is not always great.
I remember well how I felt so grand,
To act like a man with a smoke in my hand.

Yes, regretting now
Now I know my decision was wrong
What sorrows for me could tobacco bring?
That was just a childhood fling.

Years gone
And still not neglect,
A better life was offered to me
From those who care and all for free.

The life was written with pencil! I wish
So could erase and write all over again.

❑❑❑

It's When You Heartily Smile

It was tough, so tough till you came
But your appearance made it easy,
I noticed that day nothing but your smile
That charming curve on your face
Made me happy for a while.

That universal language of yours
Shows the compassion and strength in you,
You exactly look like a child
Yes, it's when you heartily smile.

What to say about the nature so calm
The simplest life you live,
And you live with the love you keep
And I can feel it, in the eyes so deep.

I know, I have spent hours
Hours thinking about you
To write something special
For someone, specially like you.

❑❑❑

It's The Jeweller In You

Your soothing smile soothes everyone,
Your deep eyes, speak without words,
I remember in every situation,
The way your head nodes.

Not just a language,
You have taught lessons for life,
Taking a glance one can predict,
How perfect you are a teacher, daughter, mother and wife.

Being a mother second,
You have taken responsibilities of a Guru first,
With your knowledge and experience,
You are quenching our thirst.

You say we are the diamonds
Among that very crowd,
But we were just stones,
The jeweller in you is Carving us out.

Will not work the frivolous words
Like Thank You!
Just want to say on this very day,
A reason for my excellence is you!

❑❑❑

Something's there in...

Inside us is present
A darker side of ours,
Something's there in
That's killing the charm.

Every now and then
When you are not you,
Something's there in
That's controlling you.

The thoughts that overpower
Every chunk of belief,
Something's there in
That's not letting me relief.

The storm of overthinking
Is always knocking high,
Something's there in
That's not letting me sigh.

The tag of validity
Why I'm in search of,
Something's there in
That's turning me off.

Receiving the ignorance
Craving for attention,
Something's there in
That's pulling me in detention.

Worn out by failures
Is there hope any more?
Something's there in
That I can't adore.

The tremble! The frustration!
That's nothing new,
Something's there in
That's nothing but you.

❑❑❑

The Canvas

Feel the texture of the leaves
Understand the flow of paints
Know the white plane well
To create a painting on
The canvas!

Assume the aroma around
Taste that quite freshness
Listen to the mixing of ideas
To put life in
The canvas!

Memorise the movements
Tackle the turns
Fight the furious

To learn something from
The canvas!

Sense the sorrow
Hire the joy
Accept the fear
To acquire love from
The canvas!

Master the art
Fabricate the masterpiece
Grasp whatever you can
Because life is like
The canvas!

❐❐❐

Don't Forget To Smile

Every morning is a new journey,
Just leave the past away
Don't forget to smile today.

Thousands of thoughts running around,
Just let the imagination to unlay
Don't forget to smile today.

People come and people go,
Just let them, consequences to pay
Don't forget to smile today.

Drop by drop falling the rain,
Just let the rain to reach midway
Don't forget to smile today.

Beauty's felt in the heart,
You're beautiful, by the way!
Don't forget to smile today.

❑❑❑

Broken Is Beautiful

The pure heart of yours
The love that you keep,
For those who keep it safe,
For those who never return,
And for those who broke
Broke the heart with love full
But don't worry,
Because broken is beautiful!

The amazing strength of yours
The way you portray it,
For those who enhance,
For those who not care,
And for those who broke
Broke the strength full

But don't worry,
Because broken is beautiful!

The self-esteem of yours
The way you nurture it,
For those who respect,
For those who embarrass,
And for those who broke
Broke the morale full
But don't worry,
Because broken is beautiful!

❑❑❑

It's not Your Fault

It's not your fault, it never was!

When they teach you not to cry
When they ask you to be bold,
And so you never try
We are weak, you are always told,
We do understand because
It's not your fault, it never was!

The way they treat us is what you learn
We can just cook is what you see,
They never look at our concern
We are never set to be free,
We do understand because
It's not your fault, it never was!

Conservatism is passed on to you
Responsibilities you have to take,
The typical mindset obstructs your view
And so the stereotype you can't break,
We do understand because
It's not your fault, it never was!

Your shoulders need some rest as well
Your eyes can cry too,
Don't judge me, I can also excel
I will not judge you too,
We do understand because
It's not your fault, it never was!

❑❑❑

They Were Just Dreams

The endless sky
Is what I adore
My heart is fabricating dreams
To my astonishment
The clouds of crystal
Are moving through my dreams
To watch the stars
My eyes never blink
But twinkling are my dreams
The crescent moon
Is so stubborn
It's smiling in my dreams
The horizon
Where the sky meets the earth
Oh!
They were just my dreams

❑❑❑

What If Words Weren't There?

The zig-zag straight lines
Are when carved into moulds,
The rings and the roofs
Becomes the jewellery then,
Holding hands when letters
Form a necklace,
Tied with friendship words grew up
Flowing through lips
They blend into thoughts.

What if words weren't there?

Words weren't there
Letters didn't existed,
No more necklaces adorning

No rings, no roofs
The friendship was broken,
The lines were lines
No moulds no carving.

What if words weren't there?

No flowing lips
No blending thoughts,
This poem
I wasn't writing,
The lines were lines
No moulds no carving.

What if words weren't there?

❏❏❏

It's Hard Earned

Smiling in the flambeau
Hiding tears in fumes,
This respect didn't just happen
It's hard earned!

What about the yacht floating in the river
What about the passerine pondering in the yacht,
Who forgot the path
To make the destination his own,
This pride didn't just happen
It's hard earned!

What about the blood shed while sweating,

What about wars
Fought within self,
Have turned nights into days
This fame didn't just happen
It's hard earned!

❑❑❑

You're Enough

The rain cannot extinguish your light,
The storm cannot deepen your fear,
The flood within you cannot devastate your faith,
Because you're enough!

They cannot doubt you,
They cannot point you,
They cannot shake your confidence,
Because you're enough!

You can fight back hard,
You can withstand that upheaval,
You can face the people,
Because you're enough!

❑❑❑

Perfectly Imperfect

Hairs not silken
Forehead too broaden
No deep eyes
No rosy lips
I'm perfectly imperfect!

Collars not shown
Curves aren't curvy
No flat waists
No proper figures
Yes, I'm perfectly imperfect!

Speech so stammering
Memory quite weak
No fancy vocabulary

No correct sentences
Yes, I'm perfectly imperfect!

Personality not so attractive
Dressing has no sense
No eye contacts
No self-faith
Yes, I'm perfectly imperfect!

Perfection isn't necessary
But imperfection is needed
A chance to improve it is
A way to be better
Yes, I'm perfectly imperfect!
Because imperfection is perfect.

❏❏❏

It's Okay

It's okay!
It's okay to sometimes cry,
It's okay to again and again try,
It's okay to be afraid,
It's okay to have fears,
It's okay to not dare,
It's okay to lose confidence,
It's okay to be nervous,
It's okay to shout,
It's okay to laugh hard at a moment,
It's okay to tremble at another,
It's okay to be rejected,
It's okay to have weird perceptions,
It's okay to be tall or to be short,
It's okay to be thin or to be fat,

It's okay to be fair or to be dark,
It's okay to be different,
It's okay to be imperfect,
It's okay to not to be okay.

❑❑❑

You Need Someone

In the world full of people
When you're lonely
You need someone,
Someone who be
Someone who stand
And someone who sit by side.

In the world full of people
When you're lonely
You need someone,
Someone who love
Someone who care
And someone who appreciate,

In the world full of people
When you're lonely
You need someone!

I've got that Someone
That someone for me
That someone in me
That someone is I.

I who stand for myself
I who sit besides myself
I who love to love myself,
I who care for my needs
I who appreciate my own dignity
I who never underestimate my potential
I have got my own self.

It is I and so are you,
I have found that someone in me,
And you should try it too.

❑❑❑

No One To Tell

Number of things
Moving in head,
But you have
No one to tell.

When closed walls
Are eating you in,
When you can't handle
The loudness out.

Screaming voices
Is all what you hear,
But no one you have
To share your fear.

The insecurities
And self doubt,
You can't cope up
With stressed outs.

No
It's just not you tho,
More people out there
Feeling the same pain,
And they too have
No one to tell.

❏❏❏